❧ THE NECESSARY CAT ❧

Pansy   Tikki

First published 1998 by Walker Books Ltd
87 Vauxhall Walk, London SE11 5HJ

10 9 8 7 6 5 4 3 2

© 1998 Nicola Bayley

Poems © individual authors as noted
in Acknowledgements

A variety of typefaces has been used in this book,
with handlettering by Annabelle Davis.

Printed in Belgium

British Library Cataloguing in Publication Data
A catalogue record for this book is available
from the British Library.

ISBN 0-7445-1924-1

✥ THE NECESSARY CAT ✥

A Celebration of Cats in Picture and Word

NICOLA BAYLEY

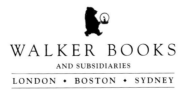

WALKER BOOKS
AND SUBSIDIARIES
LONDON • BOSTON • SYDNEY

David Ford's cats ~ THELMA & LOUISE

Particular thanks to ~
Amelia, Vanessa, Elizabeth,
Helen, Julia, Janna, Gill, Mark and Peter
for their invaluable help in preparing this book.

All my work is done in the company of cats, first Bella and now Pansy and Tikki, so when a friend of mine, David Ford, suggested that I do a book all about cats, I leapt at the idea. Little did I know that the work would take me four years, beginning by simply sifting through the myriad pieces of cat ephemera I have been collecting all my life. Then came the challenge of illustrating the poems, sayings, facts and images of cats that I had discovered. I would like to dedicate this book to David Ford but I hope it will be enjoyed by anyone who finds cats as beautiful and as necessary as I do. ~

Nicola Bayley

CONTENTS

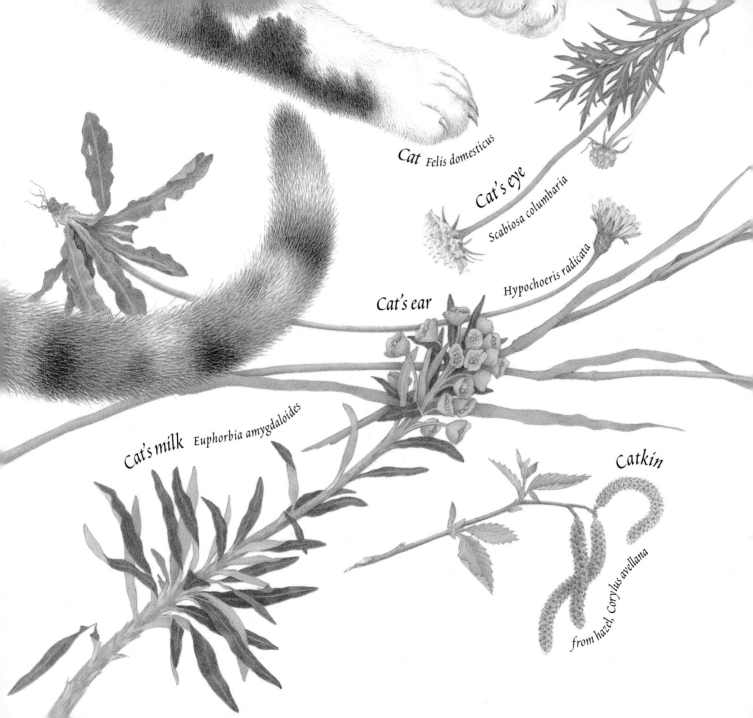

Cat *Felis domesticus*

Cat's eye *Scabiosa columbaria*

Hypochoeris radicata

Cat's ear

Cat's milk *Euphorbia amygdaloides*

Catkin

from hazel, Corylus avellana

Catnip *Nepeta cataria*

Cat locks *Eriophorum angustifolium*

Cat's claws *Lotus corniculatus*

Cat's face

Viola tricolor

The Cat's Meadow

Cat's-tail *Phleum bertolonii*

Cat's foot

Glechoma hederacea

Cat Scraps

GATÃO
PUSS IN BOOTS
VINHO VERDE
Região Demarcada
BRANCO 75CL

PRODUCT OF PORTUGAL

Chocolat POULAIN
Goûtez & Comparez

8 - Le Chat Botté

I HAVE MADE A HASH OF THINGS!

15 भारत INDIA

6

SOMETHING ON MY MIND

Copyright 1905
Rotary Photo

Mackintosh's
Nurseryland
Toffee de Luxe

MARY
CONTRARY

PUSS IN
BOOTS

tosh's
yland
e Luxe

Mac
Nu
Tof

TEA TIME

УССУРИЙСКИЙ ТИГР ПОЧТА СССР 25 КОП

THREE CATS

REG'D. TRADE MARK

Manufactured by Spruce

MADE IN ENGLAND

Kitty

PLAYING BALL

WIND UP

中國製造
MADE IN CHINA

"Got Sumthin."

THE YOUNG PRACTITIONER

Hungry Cats

JACK SPRAT

Had a cat,
It had but one ear;
It went to buy butter
When butter was dear.

RAT A TAT TAT who is that?
Only grandma's pussy cat.
What do you want?
A pint of milk.
Where's your money?
In my pocket.
Where's your pocket?
I forgot it.
Oh, you silly pussy cat!

PUSSY AT THE FIRESIDE suppin' up brose,
Down came a cinder and burned pussy's nose.
Oh, said pussy, that's no fair.
Well, said the cinder, you shouldn't be there.

HIE, HIE, SAYS ANTHONY,

Puss is in the pantry,
Gnawing, gnawing,
A mutton, mutton bone;
See how she tumbles it,
See how she mumbles it,
See how she tosses
The mutton, mutton bone.

SING, SING,

What shall I sing?
The cat's run away
With the pudding string!

Do, do,
What shall I do?
The cat's run away
With the pudding, too!

RINDLE, RANDLE,

Light the candle,
The cat's among the pies;
No matter for that,
The cat'll get fat,
And I'm too lazy to rise.

To Mrs Reynolds' Cat

Cat! who hast pass'd thy grand climacteric,
How many mice and rats hast in thy days
Destroy'd? How many tit bits stolen? Gaze
With those bright languid segments green, and prick
Those velvet ears – but pr'ythee do not stick
Thy latent talons in me – and upraise
Thy gentle mew – and tell me all thy frays,
Of fish and mice, and rats and tender chick.
Nay, look not down, nor lick thy dainty wrists –
For all thy wheezy asthma – and for all
Thy tail's tip is nick'd off – and though the fists
Of many a maid have given thee many a maul,
Still is that fur as soft, as when the lists
In youth thou enter'dest on glass bottled wall.

John Keats

From The Kitten
and Falling Leaves

—But the Kitten, how she starts,

Crouches, stretches, paws and darts!

With a tiger-leap half-way

Now she meets the coming prey,

Lets it go as fast, and then

Has it in her power again.

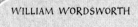

WILLIAM WORDSWORTH

the fight begins when

you pull the strings

cat marionette

wind-up cat

prrr rrr rrr

CATS IN THE TOY CUPBOARD

if you know how, you can make this cat crumple

Three Little Kittens

what fun — kitty tiddlywinks!

this tin cat has lost his key!

pull the string and pussy chases the mouse

articulated cat

22

finger puppet

cats to cuddle

tiny jigsaw cat

a cat to clutch

doll's house cats

hand puppets

shake the mouse and tease the cat

press my back to make me *miaow*

an old board game, with tiny china cat and mouse pieces on a merry chase

The New Game
"POUNCE"
FOR TWO PLAYERS
PUBLISHED BY
J. JAQUES & SON, LONDON

When in Doubt – Wash

If you have committed any kind of an error
and anyone scolds you – wash.
If you slip and fall off something
and somebody laughs at you – wash.

If somebody calls you and you
don't care to come and still you don't
wish to make it a direct insult – wash.
Something hurt you? Wash it.

Door closed and you're burning up
because no one will open it for you –
have yourself a little wash and forget it.
Someone petting another cat or dog
in the same room, and you are annoyed
over that – be nonchalant; wash.
Feel sad – wash away your blues.

And – of course you also wash
to get clean and to keep clean.

Paul Gallico

Cats Sleep

Cats sleep
Anywhere,
Any table,
Any chair,
Top of piano,
Window-ledge,
In the middle,
On the edge,
Open drawer,
Empty shoe,
Anybody's
Lap will do,
Fitted in a
Cardboard box,
In the cupboard
With your frocks –
Anywhere!
They don't care!
Cats sleep
Anywhere.

Eleanor Farjeon

The composer Champfleury claimed to hear 63 separate notes in a cat's mew.

A cat can have as many as 120,000 hairs per square inch.

The first exhibition of cats took place at Crystal Palace in London in 1871.

Did You Know That...?

Tiddles, the ladies' room cat at Paddington Station, London, weighed 32 lbs and had his own refrigerator.

No two tigers have the same markings.

"The Cat & Fiddle", a popular name for English pubs, was carelessly borrowed from the French for "The Faithful Cat", which is *Le Chat Fidèle*.

Of all cat breeds, only the cheetah cannot retract its claws.

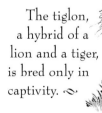

The tiglon, a hybrid of a lion and a tiger, is bred only in captivity.

Cheshire cheeses were commonly moulded into the shape of a grinning cat.

The Fishing Cat, *Felis viverrina*, has partially webbed feet.

White cats are very often deaf.

All white tigers of Rewa are descended from Mohan, who died aged 19, leaving 114 white descendants with ice-blue eyes.

It was once thought that the dung and urine of a cat could cure baldness.

The black tuft on a lion's tail conceals a claw or spur.

When a cat is frightened, it sweats through its feet.

Motherly cats will suckle otter pups.

A bottle foster mother comes in handy for an orphaned kitten.

The Savoy Hotel in London employs Kaspar, a wooden cat in dinner dress, to be the fourteenth guest for parties of thirteen – thus avoiding bad luck!

The paws of *Felis bieti*, the Chinese Desert Cat, are very hairy to protect them from the hot sand.

The author's cat loves melon and beetroot.

Bella Counts to Ten

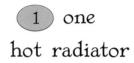

1 one
hot radiator

2 two
strong brushes

3 three
warm lights

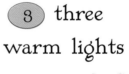

4 four
willing laps

5 five
favourite plants

6 six
different dishes

29

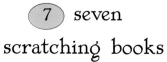 **7** seven
scratching books

8 eight
fat mice

9 nine
tangly balls

30

10 ten
small birds

Cat Lore

*A bashful cat makes
a proud mouse.*

❖

*The cat with a straw tail
keeps away from fire.*

*Don't let the cat
out of the bag.*

❖

*It's raining
cats and dogs.*

*The dog wakes three times
to watch over its master;
The cat wakes three times
to strangle him.*

*When the cats go off,
the mice go dancing.*

❖

*Gloved cats catch
no mice.*

*A scalded cat
dreads cold water.*

❖

*He's as honest as the cat
when the meat's out of reach.*

*A dab of lard
cures all, even
the cat's boil.*

❖

*Rub a cat's paw
with butter, and
it will not stray.*

❖

She that denies
the cat skimmed
milk must give
the mouse cream.

Kiss the black cat,
t'will make ye fat;
Kiss the white one,
t'will make ye lean.

Whenever the cat
of the house is black,
the lasses of lovers
will have no lack.

A ship's cat that's black
brings bad luck;
a tortoiseshell cat
brings good.

There'll be no playing
with straw
before an old cat.

A halfpenny cat
may look at a king.

Curiosity
killed the cat.

A cat will never drown
if it can see the shore.

There's more than one
way to skin a cat.

There's not room
to swing a cat.

The cat sees through
shut lids.

Fourteen Ways of Touching the Peter

George MacBeth

I

You can push
your thumb
in the
ridge
between his
shoulder-blades
to please him.

II

Starting
at its root,
you can let
his whole
tail
flow
through your hand.

III

Forming
a fist
you can let
him rub
his bone
skull
against it, hard.

IV

When he makes
bread,
you can lift
him
by his under-
sides on your
knuckles.

V

In hot
weather
you can itch
the fur
under
his chin. He
likes that.

VI

At night
you can hoist
him
out of his bean-stalk,
sleepily
clutching
paper bags.

35

VII

Pressing
his head against
your cheek,
you can carry
him
in the dark,
safely.

VIII

In late Autumn
you can find
seeds
adhering
to his fur.
There are
plenty.

IX

You can prise
his jaws
open,
helping
any medicine
he won't
abide, go down.

X

You can touch
his
feet, only
if
he is relaxed.
He
doesn't like it.

XI

You can comb
spare thin
fur
from his coat,
so he won't
get
fur-ball.

XII

You can shake
his rigid
chicken-leg leg,
scouring his
hind-quarters
with his Vim
tongue.

XIII

Dumping
hot fish
on his plate, you can
fend
him off,
pushing
and purring.

XIV

You can have
him shrimp
along you,
breathing,
whenever
you want
to compose poems.

Exotic Cats

1 Japanese Bobtail

2 Sphynx

3 Egyptian Mau

4 Turkish Van

5 Birman

6 Devon Rex

7 Scottish Fold

8 Odd-eyed Angora

Catfish

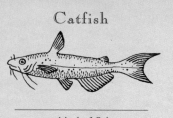

a kind of fish

Cat's tongues

a meagre meal

Cat's ice

a thin layer of ice

Catboat

a small sailing boat

Cathead

a wooden bracket on a ship

Cat

Cat stand

always lands upright

Cat-stick

an Elizabethan bat for tip-cat

Cat's-head

an architectural moulding

Cat's-brains

patterns in sandstone

Cat's-paw

a gentle breeze

Catgut

strings made from sheep gut

Cat stane

a conical cairn

Catbird

an American thrush

Cat-stitch

a needlework outline

Cat's-cradle

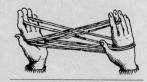

a game played with string

Cat's-eye

polished quartz

Cat-hauling

a harsh punishment

Cat's-whisker

a brass wire in early radios

Catcall	Cat snake	Cat castle	Catnap

a mouth instrument for squealing	a large snake	a wheeled shield	a short snooze

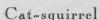

Cat-squirrel			Cat's hairs
	**Words** 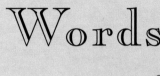		
a kind of racoon			sores and corns

Cat block	Cat's-head	Cat-o'-nine-tails	Cat-ogle
		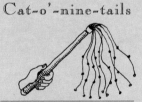	
a large block or pully	a type of apple	a flogging device	a large hooting owl

Cat's hair	Cat-shark	Cat-skin	Cat-face

down on a young boy's face	a kind of spotted shark	an inferior silk hat	an ornate carving on a chair

Catspaw	Cat crane	Cat-lap	Cat-o'-two-tails

irregular marbling	a davit on a ship's deck	a weak drink	an earwig

THE LION

The Lion, the Lion, he dwells in the waste,
He has a big head and a very small waist;
But his shoulders are stark,
and his jaws they are grim,
And a good little child
will not play with
him.

THE TIGER

The Tiger on the other hand, is kittenish and mild,

He makes a pretty playfellow for any little child;

And mothers of large families

(who claim to common sense)

Will find a Tiger well repays

the trouble and expense.

HILAIRE BELLOC

Three young rats with black felt hats,
Three young ducks with white straw flats,
Three young dogs with curling tails,
Three young cats with demi-veils,
Went out to walk with two young pigs
In satin vests and sorrel wigs;
But suddenly it chanced to rain
And so they all went home again.

Higglety, pigglety, pop!
The dog has eaten the mop;
The pig's in a hurry,
The cat's in a flurry,
Higglety, pigglety, pop!

Nonsensical

Hoddley, poddley, puddle and fogs,
   Cats are to marry the poodle dogs;
Cats in blue jackets and dogs in red hats,
What will become of the mice and the rats?

Cats

Distinguished Cats

Sugar, the cat who walked 1,500 miles from California to Oklahoma, USA, in order to rejoin her family

Pepper, the motion picture cat, who starred alongside Charlie Chaplin

Mourka, the cat of Stalingrad, who during World War II delivered vital messages from Russian scouts about enemy gun emplacements

Wilberforce, the cat who lived in Downing Street from 1973-1988, through the rule of four prime ministers

Towzer, a champion ratter who killed 28,899 rats over 24 years while employed at the Glen Turret distillery on Tayside, Scotland

Snowball, the cat who helped lay cable for the Grand-Coulee Dam in Washington state, USA, by dragging a cable through bent piping

Fat Albert, the official blood donor for the cats of New Jersey, USA

Scarlett, the cat who ran into a burning house in New York five times to save her litter of kittens

Mike, the British Museum cat, who greeted visitors there for more than nineteen years

Simon, the captain's cat, who was given the Dickin Medal in 1949 for bravery in protecting food supplies on the HMS Amethyst

47

Quorum Porum

In a dark Garden, by a dreadful Tree,

The Druid Toms were met. They numbered three:

Tab Tiger, Demon Black, and Ginger Hate.

Their forms were tense, their eyes were full of fate.

Save for the involuntary caudal thrill,

The horror was that they should sit so still.

An hour of ritual silence passed: then low

And marrow-freezing, Ginger moaned OROW,

Two horrid syllables of hellish lore,

Followed by deeper silence than before.

Another hour, the tabby's turn is come:

Rigid, he rapidly howls MUM MUM MUM,

Then reassumes his silence like a pall,

Clothed in negation, a dumb oracle.

At the third hour, the Black gasps out AH BLURK

Like a lost soul that founders in the mirk,

And the grim, ghastly, damned, and direful crew

Resumes its voiceless vigilance anew.

The fourth hour passes. Suddenly all three
Chant WEGGY WEGGY WEGGY mournfully,
Then stiffly rise, and melt into the shade,
Their Sabbath over, and their demons laid.

Ruth Pitter

About 50 million years ago, the first ancestor of the cat appeared: the weasel-like Miacid.

In 500 BC, Persian soldiers carried cats into battle to protect themselves from the Egyptians, who were loath to harm the sacred animal.

At the turn of the 19th century, 300,000 mummified cats were unearthed in Beni Hasan, Egypt. Most were sent to England to be used as fertilizer.

HISTORICAL

Bastet, the Ancient Egyptian goddess of life, maternity and happiness, was also known as Pasht, from which "puss" is possibly derived.

Ancient Egyptians shaved off their eyebrows to mourn the death of a cat.

The Japanese revered cats for protecting their precious silkworms from mice. The cat statues at Gokoku-ji temple in Tokyo raise their paws for good luck.

Ancient Romans made sure to nod respectfully to passing cats for fear of being cursed with the "evil eye".

In the Middle Ages, people believed that witches could change into feline form – but only nine times.

In the 16th century, Prussian soldiers used "fire-cats", explosives strapped to their backs, to spread fire in enemy quarters.

ODDMENTS

St Agatha and St Gertrude are among several saints who are associated with cats. St Jerome is always depicted with his tame lion.

Dick Whittington's cat may not have been a cat at all, but the cat-boat that carried the coal that made the man's fortune.

Despite the fear and superstition surrounding the cat in the Middle Ages, its image was frequently featured in church carvings.

In medieval times, the herb rue was tied beneath the wings of chicks to repel hungry cats.

Up until the 18th century, a cat was often walled up in a newly built house to keep the devil – and the rats – away.

Five Eyes

 In Hans' old mill his three black cats
Watch the bins for thieving rats.
Whisker and claw, they crouch in the night,
Their five eyes smouldering green and bright:
Squeaks from the flour sacks, squeaks from where
The cold wind stirs on the empty stair,
Squeaking and scampering everywhere.
Then down they pounce, now in, now out,
At whisking tail, and sniffing snout;
While lean old Hans he snores away
Till peep of light at break of day;
Then up he climbs to his creaking mill,
Out comes his cats all grey with meal –
Jekkel, and Jessup, and one-eyed Jill.

Walter de la Mare

GOYA

CHU LING

GALLERY CATS

ROUSSEAU

PAINTED IN
HOMAGE TO THE WORLD'S
GREAT ARTISTS

FLEMISH MASTER
(NAME UNKNOWN)

BARTOLL

CHARDIN

BOSCH

HOGARTH

BRUEGHEL
THE ELDER

LOTTO

LEYSTER

MOSLER

PEALE

GOSHUN

DOMENICHINO

STEINLEN

PINTORICCHIO

HALL OF FAME

CATS FROM LITERATURE, NEWSPRINT AND THE MOVING SCREEN

from left to right, top to bottom

TOM (*appearing tonight without* **Jerry**)

KATHLEEN HALE'S **ORLANDO** THE **MARMALADE CAT**

A LOUIS WAIN **TOFF** ✦ NICOLA BAYLEY'S **PATCHWORK CAT**

THE DANDY'S **KORKY** ✦ BEATRIX POTTER'S **TOM KITTEN**

FELIX THE CAT ✦ EDWARD GOREY'S **AMPHIGOREY CAT**

JOHN TENNIEL'S **CHESHIRE CAT**

EDWARD LEAR'S **FOSS** ✦ E.H. SHEPARD'S **TIGGER**

On a Night of Snow

Cat, if you go outdoors, you must walk in the snow.
   You will come back with little white shoes on your feet,
little white shoes of snow that have heels of sleet.
   Stay by the fire, my Cat. Lie still, do not go.
See how the flames are leaping and hissing low,
   I will bring you a saucer of milk like a marguerite,
so white and so smooth, so spherical and so sweet —
   stay with me, Cat. Outdoors the wild winds blow.

Outdoors the wild winds blow, Mistress, and dark is the night,
   strange voices cry in the trees, intoning strange lore,
and more than cats move, lit by our eyes' green light,
   on silent feet where the meadow grasses hang hoar —
Mistress, there are portents abroad of magic and might,
   and things that are yet to be done. Open the door!

Elizabeth Coatsworth

Cats Can Be...

Alien

Bashful

Cunning

Dim

Enormous

Foolish

Glorious

Hairy

Idle

Jolly

Kindly

Lean

Magical

Obstinate

Naughty

Proud

Quiet

Ridiculous

Talented

Silly

62

Unfortunate

Valuable

Worrying

Xenophobic

Yowly

Zealous

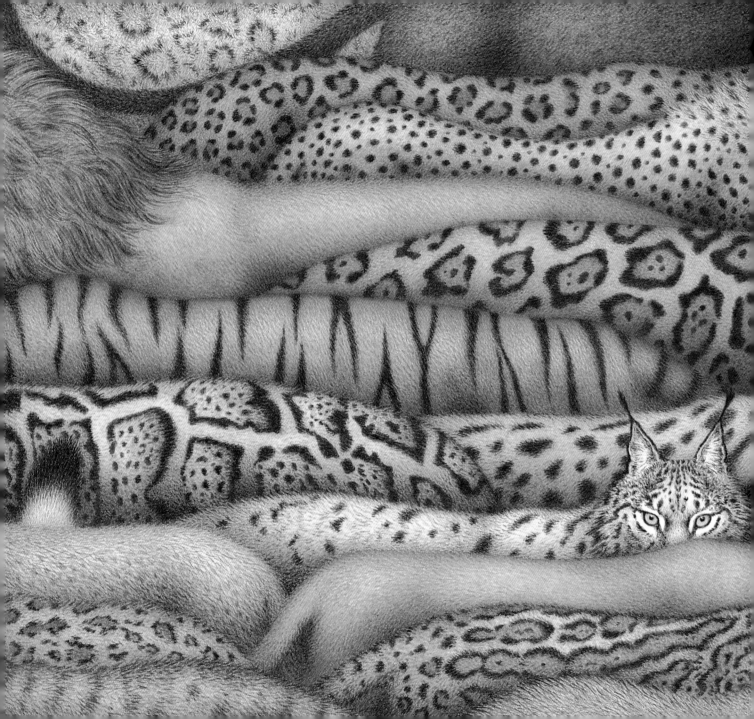

Lion

Tiger

Panther

Clouded Leopard

Wild
C A T S

Snow Leopard

Caracal

Jaguar

Leopard

Cheetah

Lynx

Bobcat

Ocelot

Serval

Margay

Wild Cat

Sand Cat

65

Famous People

SIR ISAAC NEWTON

1642–
1727

Newton, known best for his theory of gravitation, is thought to have invented the cat flap.

SIR WINSTON CHURCHILL

1874–
1965

Churchill praised the war effort of his cat Nelson: "He acts as a hot-water bottle and saves fuel, power and energy!"

SAMUEL JOHNSON

1709–
1784

Dr Johnson insisted that his beloved Hodge should dine upon nothing but oysters.

EDWARD LEAR

1812–
1888

Lear built a carbon copy of his house when he moved so that his ancient tabby, Foss, would always feel at home.

COLETTE

1873–
1954

Colette declared that "our perfect companions never have fewer than four feet".

THEODORE ROOSEVELT
1858–1919

Roosevelt's cat, Slippers, always attended
the President's official White House dinners.

SIR HENRY WYAT
DIED 1154

Wyat's cat saved him from starvation in the Tower of
London by bringing him pigeons to eat.

FLORENCE NIGHTINGALE
1820–1910

Nightingale, famous for her treatment of wounded
soldiers, also took cats under her wing – more than sixty!

ERNEST HEMINGWAY
1899–1961

Hemingway admired cats for their "absolute emotional
honesty". At one time he lived with thirty cats.

WILLIAM BUTLER YEATS
1865–1939

Yeats cut a piece from his fur coat rather than disturb the
resident cat of the Abbey Theatre in Dublin.

and Their Cats

On a Cat,
Ageing

He blinks upon the hearth-rug,
And yawns in deep content,
Accepting all the comforts
That Providence has sent.

Louder he purrs, and louder,
In one glad hymn of praise
For all the night's adventures,
For quiet, restful days.

Life will go on for ever,
With all that cat can wish:
Warmth and the glad procession
Of fish and milk and fish.

Only ~ the thought disturbs him ~
He's noticed once or twice,
The times are somehow breeding
A nimbler race of mice.

Alexander Gray

71

Unfortunate Cats

DING, DONG, BELL,

Pussy's in the well.

Who put her in?

Little Johnny Green.

Who pulled her out?

Little Tommy Stout.

What a naughty boy was that

To try to drown

Poor pussy cat,

Who never did him any harm,

And killed the mice

In his father's barn.

PUSSY-CAT, PUSSY-CAT, where are you going?

"Into the meadow to see the men mowing."

If you go there you are sure to be shot,

Put in a pudding, and boiled in a pot.

LINGLE, LINGLE, lang tang,

Our cat's dead!

What did she die with?

With a sore head!

All you that kent her,

When she was alive,

Come to her burial,

Atween four and five.

Cat of Cats

Now Tom's translated, not a mouse
    Dare inhabit Heaven's house;
Cherubim shall bring him milk,
    Seraphs stroke his coat of silk
While, with whiskers aureoled,
    He shall walk the streets of gold
Or, happily relaxed, lie prone,
    Deeply purring, by the throne.

Vivien Bulkley

~ Index of Titles and First Lines ~

~ Acknowledgements ~

For permission to reprint poems we would like to thank: The Peters Fraser and Dunlop Group Ltd on behalf of The Estate of Hilaire Belloc for "The Lion" and "The Tiger" from *Cautionary Verses* by **Hilaire Belloc**; Mark Paterson and Associates on behalf of The Estate of Elizabeth Coatsworth for "On a Night of Snow" © 1926 **Elizabeth Coatsworth**; The Literary Trustees of **Walter de la Mare**, and the Society of Authors as their representative, for "Five Eyes" from *The Complete Poems of Walter de la Mare* (1969); David Higham Associates for "Cats Sleep" from *The Children's Bells* by **Eleanor Farjeon** (Oxford University Press); Aitken & Stone Ltd for "When in Doubt – Wash" from *The Abandoned* © 1950 **Paul Gallico**; John Gray for "On a Cat, Ageing" by **Alexander Gray**; Sheil Land Associates Ltd for "Fourteen Ways of Touching the Peter" from *The Night of Stones* by **George MacBeth** (Secker & Warburg, 1968); Enitharmon Press for "Quorum Porum" from *Collected Poems* by **Ruth Pitter** (1996); and A P Watt Ltd on behalf of Michael Yeats for "The Cat and the Moon" by **W.B. Yeats** from *The Collected Works of W.B. Yeats*.

Permission to illustrate the cats in "Hall of Fame" was granted by: Donadio & Ashworth Inc. for "Amphigorey Cat" © 1972 Edward Gorey; King Features Syndicate Inc. for "Felix the Cat" © 1992; D.C. Thomson & Co. Ltd for "Korky" from "The Dandy"; Frederick Warne for "Orlando the Marmalade Cat" © Kathleen Hale and for Beatrix Potter's "Tom Kitten"; Trustees of the Pooh Properties, the Executor of E.H. Shepard and the E.H. Shepard Trust for "Tigger" from *The House at Pooh Corner* by A.A. Milne, drawn from the original illustration by E.H. Shepard; and Turner Entertainment Co. for use of the "Tom & Jerry" cartoon characters, all rights reserved.

Permission to paint details from works by the masters in "Gallery Cats" was given by courtesy of: The National Gallery, London, for **William Hogarth**, "The Graham Children", **Domenichino**, "Apollo Killing the Cyclops", **Pintoricchio**, "Penelope with the Suitors", and **Judith Leyster**, "A Boy and a Girl"; Abby Aldrich Rockefeller Folk Art Center, Williamsburg, Virginia, USA, for **W.T. Bartoll**, "Girl and Cat"; The Kunsthaus Zurich for **Henri Rousseau**, "Portrait of Pierre Loti", © 1997 Kunsthaus Zurich, all rights reserved; The Pinacoteca Comunale di Recanati for **Lorenzo Lotto**, "Annunciazione"; The Staatliche Museen zu Berlin Preussischer Kulturbesitz, Gemäldegalerie, for **Pieter Brueghel the Elder**, "Netherlandish Proverbs"; The Museo del Prado for **Hieronymus Bosch**, "The Garden of Earthly Delights"; The National Portrait Gallery, London, for **C.W. Peale**, "Charles Waterton, Naturalist 1824"; and The Metropolitan Museum of Art, New York, for **Matsumura Goshun**, "Seated Cat": Rogers Fund, 1971 (1971.190), **Henry Mosler**, "Just Moved": Arthur Hoppock Hearn Fund, 1962 (62.80), **Jean Baptiste Siméon Chardin**, "The Silver Tureen": Fletcher Fund, 1959 (59.9), **Master of the Story of Joseph**, "Joseph Interpreting the Dreams of His Fellow Prisoners": Harris Brisbane Dick Fund, 1953 (53.168), **Francisco Goya**, "Don Manuel Osorio Manrique de Zuñiga": The Jules Bache Collection, 1949 (49.7.41), **Chu Ling**, "Seated Cat": Rogers Fund, 1956 (56.129.3), and **Théophile Alexandre Steinlen**, "Compagnie Française des Chocolats et des Thés": Gift of Bessie Potter Vonnoh, 1941 (41.12.19).

Every effort has been made to secure permission for use of copyrighted material. If notified of any omission, the editor and publisher will gladly make the necessary correction in future printings.